"How do I write good Instagram captions that don't sound like an ad?"

Sometimes coming up with good Instagram captions can be really, really hard. Some days creativity flows like a fine wine and other days, the writer's block is for real! Whether you're just starting an Instagram brand page or looking for new ideas, I have developed this handbook full of bulletproof Instagram caption ideas that can spark creativity and put your captions on auto-pilot.

Hi, I'm Oliver Swig and firstly I'd like to personally thank you for downloading this e-book. I would like to say up-front that I am not a marketing guru or even a social media copywriter. "I just bought your book, why are you telling me this." you ask? Well, I am a marketing veteran that has worked in the social media and branding space for over ten years and throughout my career, I have always struggled coming up with new content ideas. Ideas that have great engagement by injecting personality and inspire my client's followers to take action. I wondered if there was an easier way, a hack, a perfect formula or a bible full of great ideas I could use over and over again. So, over the years, I have collected an essential list of high performing captions that I use to remix, reshuffle, and write posts that always come out feeling fresh. I am excited to now make my caption templates public! For me, these ideas have served as a golden handbook that I keep coming back to time and time again. I hope that they inspire, elevate and grow your brands Instagram too!

This collection of 100 field-tested caption ideas are designed to grab your followers attention and hook new ones. These captions are flexible for all industries and strike the perfect balance of connecting with your audience and doing some self-promotion at the same time (without a hard sell). Start adding more value to your posts, build a real emotional and honest connection to your audience and drive even more engagement today!

So what does a great Instagram caption look like?

These days, people crave more from the brands they like. No one likes the hard sell. They want to be spoken to like a human. They also want **an experience**. A connection. This is what building brand value is all about. Show them why you or your brand is different **with** your own thoughts and insights. Simply put, a great Instagram caption is one that provides context, meaning, injects personality, and inspires your followers to do something.

Whatever your goal, approach your copywriting from the perspective of adding value. You are the pro, so give your followers something they cannot find anywhere else. Bring some lifestyle commentary into the conversation. Have fun too! Instagram can be a place for you to show the witty and modern side of your brand. Give some insight into what it's like behind the scenes, what it's like to work with you and ultimately...buy from you.

💡 TIP

I have noticed that of the most common reasons people have difficulty writing Instagram captions is because they try to do it on the fly, which isn't ideal. You shouldn't rush the copywriting process. Instead, schedule and plan your Instagram posts by writing them in advance using a scheduling software like later.com or the Preview app for iOS. Take the time to write (and rewrite!) them when you're in a creative mood.

Technically Speaking: Why a good Instagram caption is important.

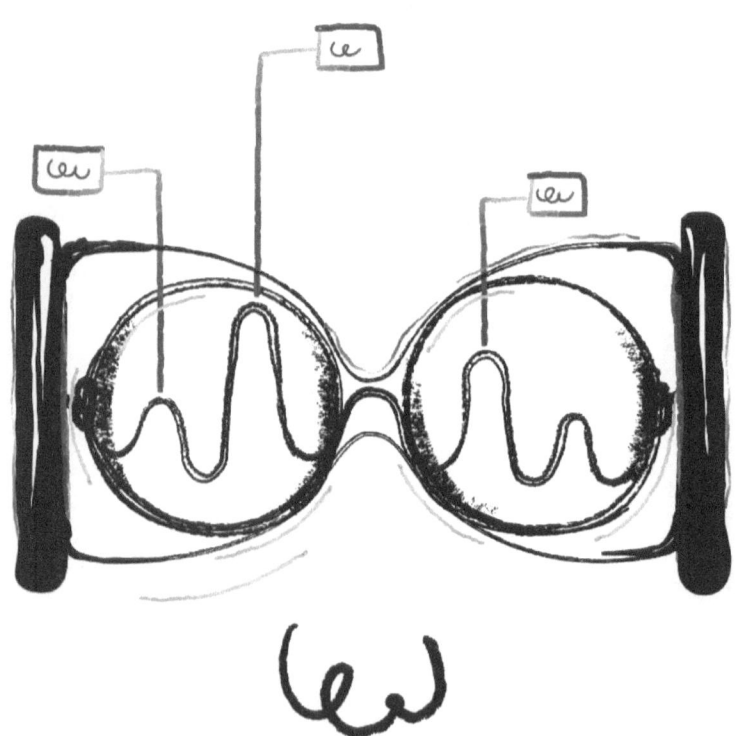

The latest iteration of the Instagram algorithm promotes posts that get a lot of engagement. When an image receives a lot of likes, comments, and shares, it tells Instagram that it is high-quality content and is probably something that other users might want to see. It works behind the scenes bumping up the post on recommended feeds for more visibility.

Writing good Instagram captions with compelling call-to-actions (CTAs) is one of the best ways to inspire your followers to like and comment on your posts, which will help boost even more engagement on your account. This book will help you come up with great ideas.

BTS (Behind The Scenes)

1. We're so excited to share with you guys what [we are working on/creating/we've got planned] - interested? We'll let you in on a / Here's a sneak peek. Any ideas? / guesses?

2. Today we found another perk of our office...A rooftop that offers prime [activity/cool thing] e.g.solar eclipse viewing!(post a roof pic)

3. Today we are #OOO/off-site and decided to work out of the [cafe, favorite place]. With a [favorite cocktail? Beer? Burger?] in hand. As you can probably guess, we are in heaven right now.

4. [@employee] and our [@otheremployee] caught accidentally #twinning at the office today. Both wearing [#brandname] (Turtlenecks, jeans, pants suits etc...) #greatminds

5. Social media is over-saturated with perfectly curated, retouched images with precise angles and ideal settings. We want to show you something REAL. A raw #BTS shot of [your brand] in action. #nofilter #noBS

6. You know how some people have a particularly captivating presence? They walk into a room and take up space without any words. Meet [employee]. That's the impact that [employee] has. When they first started with us, we thought [insert what you thought]. It looks like we did something right.

7. Can you hear me now? [@employee] (Post a photo of

an employee looking like a BOSS at their desk. Get creative e.g. they are on the phone with sunglasses juggling a sparkling water and a stack of print outs.)

8. New CONTENT on the blog! For our new content series [blog series/title], [Guest name] @guestname let us into [their office, kitchen, bedroom, house etc...] to discuss [Topic], and what she/he [another topic e.g. what he/she does in their spare time] [Pull quote e.g. "Home cooking is more about the effort," he/she says. "Perfection will come over time."] Tap the link in bio to learn more.

9. Found a pretty great work/hang/coffee/lunch chill spot yesterday and enjoyed the crap out of it with [@person1], [@person2], and [@person3]. I'll be back with my laptop and mediocre dad jokes ASAP.

10. Ladies and gents. Presenting: [Get creative with some Behind The Scenes (BTS) images. For moms, try a toddler wearing a pair of glasses with at a computer doing spreadsheets? Dogs in the office helping pack some product? Experiment!] Our newest recruits/interns at [your brand]. Do you guys think we should keep them/him/her?

11. The past few [days, months] have been an incredible adventure in all things bold and fearless. We spent months collaborating with [partner, friend, brand] to [create/curate] a group of remarkable leaders for [brand, company] pushing the boundaries of what is possible.

12. We/I came to the [trade show/event] looking for a [product/car/something cool]. But we/I might've found something else for everyday use...(Pair with an absurd

photo from the event)

13. We're not big fans of résumés. If someone wants to work at [your brand/company], we ask them to make something and show us. That's why [@person] TOTALLY blew our f**cking minds. I think he/she deserves an interview, no? (Show an impressive act of **self promotion** from a prospective employee.)

14. Taking care of the finishing touches. (Post a cherry on top type picture, something almost finished to build excitement or intrigue)

15. Bumpin' at work with our fearless [job title] [@employee] (Post a pregnant employee)

16. Someone's working late/after hours again. (Show a picture of an office dog/cat/kid in the office. @ **them** if they have an account! Post it at night or over the weekend.)

Getting personal

17. One of the biggest lessons that we've learned over the years as small business/brand owners in [industry e.g. tech,] [Challenge - e.g. Taking the time to recharge is so important.] Because you know what? [Say why]

18. Our [CTO/CFO/any employee position works] [@employee] paid a visit to [somewhere interesting e.g. art show, event] in [location]. [Fun fact about the show] #moodboard

19. Our founder/I/[employee name] actually [Something that not many people know about this person?]. You heard it here first.

20. LET'S PLAY: Two truths and a lie: [Insert two truths, one lie - get the audience to guess]. Let's see how well you know us.

21. Strictly business class. (Post a BTS photo that conveys both the luxuries and the joys of your office culture)

22. If you told me/us 5 years ago that we would be [what you do, who to], we would be like [what would you have said?]. Because here's the thing. [why? What happened to have made you say/think that?]

23. Here's a little origin story about the team. When I/our founder/[employee] grew up, she/he wanted to be a [what did they want to be?] She/He was [skills he/she exemplifies], and it just made sense. But then [something that happened that didn't end up leading him/her to that

path]. It wasn't easy. [Go through the challenges and how you/he/she overcame it].

24. I/We will never forget our first sale. We were/I was thinking: [What were your thoughts/feelings e.g. Someone actually wants to buy from me?]. The person who purchased/came to me needed [what was the job brief, or if it's a product, what did they buy?]. We'll never forget it.

25. [Describe one big challenge/obstacle you have faced in business/life?] When it happened, a lot of thoughts were floating around my/our head(s): [question you asked yourself]? [another question you asked yourself]? But you know what? [How you/the brand overcame it] [How you're better now because of it.]

💡 TIP

Always have a reason to post. Your audience craves an honest and genuine discussion. They don't want to be sold things or served up ads. They don't want to follow an account that resembles a bot. Give them a reason to support you and what you're about.

Sprinkle some value.

26. #AMA time! Alright, you guys. We are opening up the floodgates for the next hour. Our founder has agreed to respond to all of your questions about [what the brand is known for]. Are you ready? Cause we are. Hit us with your questions below. [This option would work great as an announcement for an Instagram Live also!]

27. We are brewing up something exciting. But we need your help. [A question to followers to see what they want]. What do you guys think? We are going to collate your responses and turn it into [a Value Add/Blog/Resource]. So keep those eyes peeled!

28. [SERVICE] Ok. We are spilling the beans. Want a tip on how to [sky rocket/combat/conquer] [what your brand is known to do]? Check our blog.

29. We chatted with [Another brands co-founder/CFO/important person name] [@person] about how he/she finds inspiration in [their work/life/etc]. Read via link in bio.

30. So. We are frequently asked about our favorite [insert industry] tools to manage our client's/organizing our [insert service], streamline processes and boost our productivity. One of our favorites? [insert tool]. Not only does it [what it does] but it also [what it does] and [what it does]. Um. Can we get a heck yes? We threw down 5 more of our favorite tools in our recent blog post. Link in bio.

31. We've been seeing a bit of chatter lately on the gram about [what is something that has been talked about a lot

in your industry]. Here's what we think: [what are your personal insights on this in your own words?]32. We've put together a killer list of industry trends for [year] on our blog. What have you noticed getting popular this year? Link in bio.

33. Everyone loves to use the words "disruptive" and "unexpected" but, very few brands have the guts to stand by them. (Tell a story on how you/your company was trying to be unexpected and it backfired. What was the valuable lesson learned?)

34. We're catching feelings for our [product] this season  Where would you [use, create] in your home? #TellUs below! Be sure to tune in tomorrow - we're sharing something extra special on our blog!

35. Want to know how to [make/conquer/boost][something your brand does]? If you're curious - this is just one of the topics questions our founder [@founder] answers during our #instagramlive takeover! Catch it #LIVE at 3:30PM EST / 12:30PM PST [@brand]

36. [@follower] Using our [product name]. What do you guys think? Did she/he kill it? (Try and choose an interesting photo and @ the customer)

💡 TIP

No matter how short or simple, people love being told stories. Because of this, we tend to remember and recall things better. It's memory power. Try and deliver a fact or insight in the form of a story. Take your reader on a journey.

Drive more engagement

37. We're streetcasting for our next campaign celebrating those who are working hard, and doing things their way. DM us your best headshot to get in the mix!

38. #[image subject]goals Like if you agree.

39. You asked, we answered. [Brand / Company names] limited-edition [new offering/product name] is back in stock. This might be our final run of [product name] with this special [attribute] — stock up!

40. You guys. Check this out [link/@] - so much good stuff in here ain here. Perfect for those [who is it designed for] and we just know you will love it.

41. Share stories of how [product/brand] has changed your life 👆.

42. Tag a friend/colleague who does this.

43. Tag some awesome Instagram accounts that we should be following right now. We're always on the lookout for new inspiration.

44. 🚫 What's a social media trend that needs to go away? 🚷

45. A OR B? WHICH WOULD YOU CHOOSE? Such a tough call 😬 (Post an image asking your audience to make a A or B choice. Make it related to your brand.)

46. 👀 iSPY... A GIVEAWAY 👀 Comment with how many [products] you find, and we'll pick one winner tomorrow who gets a grab bag of goodies. (Use a photo with your product hidden inside of it.)

47. Ok you guys. Be honest here. Who wore it best? Comment 👆 [Insert two pictures - don't be afraid to be a little silly here!]

48. #[Store, place] looking good Where should we go next? (Visit a store, place or agency that you or your brand admires and give them a shout out!)

49. It's time for our office playlist to be updated / We're working on a new office Spotify playlist. Who should we add on there? Comment ur fav new songs/artists below - interesting/up and coming only! (Follow up with a post to the public playlist in bio!)

50. Stop scrolling right now. Ever find yourself going down a rabbit hole of social media? Beautiful things, beautiful places. We love to compare ourselves with others in the industry. Leave one positive thing you have done or accomplished this week below!

51. 🛍 GIVEAWAY TIME 🛍 We fell in love with [another brands product] from [other brand] earlier this year, and we're finally sharing the love. We've teamed up with [other brand] One lucky winner will receive a full set of [other brands product] + [your product] of their choice. To enter, like this post, follow both [@otherbrand] and [your @], and tag a friend who loves [other brands product] in the comments below. Good luck! 🍀

52. You guys. We need your help! Tell us. What do you think about [something you would love your audience's opinion on.]

53. Stepping into friday like..#TGIF. Tell us what you got going on this weekend. We at [Your Brand?] We're going [What you'll be doing.]

54. Friday mood. (Post a ridiculous/exciting picture. Better if it relates in someway to your product/company.)

55. Current read: [Book title] // What are YOU guys reading at the moment? Share it below *got a pen and paper ready to write down your recommends*

56. Anyone else sometimes feel overwhelmed in the mornings? Maybe you have around 142534 unopened emails and 200 tabs open by 9am too?? Lately we have been trying this [tip for productivity and focus]. It works wonders! What do you guys do to stay productive/focus?

57. Check back tomorrow AM 👀 (Show a sneak peek teaser photo of your product. Follow up the next day with a reveal. Make it a new feature or never before seen addition to your product.)

💡 TIP

Always, always, ALWAYS respond to questions and comments. Followers love good discourse. They want to know you are human and not some faceless corporation (even if you are speaking from the viewpoint of a company or brand). Always be sure to stay consistent with your brand voice. Speak to them, give them the power to express their opinions, themselves, and engage with them!

Promote without sounding like an ad!

58. All sold out of our limited-edition [product], but we're hanging onto a few for you. 🖤 Tag a friend who would want one below. Picking winners tomorrow! [🕐 use a clock emoji to subtly leak/hint at the time.]

59. Looking at the world through the eyes of [a person who is interviewed.] - who was gracious enough to share his/her thoughts around work and craft with us. Our equally brilliant [job title e.g. social media director][@interviewee] interviewed her/him, and it's now live on our site.

60. DON'T MISS THIS ONE! Untill [date], relax with a complimentary [value offer] on our new website. Oh and were serving the good stuff. Walk-in or book now! Link in bio.

61. 🌟 Restock alert 🌟 [product] are finally back in stock on the site. Thanks for your patience. Now go get 'em.

62. We're a big fans of [@otherbrand], so I/we where thrilled that [@otherbrand] asked me/us to come on and share our [story e.g. career transition] Link in bio!

63. Recently, [brand] approached us because they needed some help with [what they approached you for]. Not going to lie, we were secretly beaming inside when they asked. Of course, we remained cool. Check this

pic/link in bio, for what we've been getting up to with the team.

64. The reviews are in: [a positive testimonial from a customer or client e.g."Bought this for my boyfriend, then bought it for every man in my life cause it smells so good"] | Read more about our products at [yourwebsite.com]

65. "[Testimonial]" BRB. Blushing over here! Thanks so much[Client], it was so crazy fun [what you helped them with].

66. Actual photo of what it feels like to [work with us, use our product, etc.] (Use a amazing, absurd, or vibey photo.)

67. Don't be shy. If you're just starting out or own your own business, [Your Brand] is there for you. DM to learn more about our products/brand.

68. Just one thing:[product] has arrived.

69. Hobbies: Unboxing (Show an unboxing photo of your product, make it fun.)

70. Fresh for the new [month/year] : [brand product] are restocked tomorrow. Get first dibs. It's here for a limited time only.

71. Just to clear things up, new [product] has arrived.

72. So we recently went down a rabbit hole of [content]. Usually, this series of [insert content] are reserved for our [subscribers/paying clients] but we felt it was too keep for ourselves. If you're interested in [topic], shoot us your email below and we'll send it to you, now!

73. [Post a customer review quote e.g. "Best. Gift. Ever. Can't wait to bust these babies open!"] [@imagecredit]
(Pair with an unboxing photo from a customer)

74. You're ready for [product], but is your [product], ready for you? (Post an image of someone using your product incorrectly or in a funny way)

75. Tonight's [#special day/holiday] plan: celebrate our [friends/gals/family/coworkers] with a lasagna. Recipe via our bio link.

76. New [Product] is back in stock. You know what to do.

77. Spotted: [Product] in the wild. (Re-post a photo of your product being used by a customer)

78. This is what we strive for: raising awareness for [#somethingyourbrandstandsfor] | Learn more about our products & visit [yourwebsite.com]

💡 TIP

A general rule of thumb is to post up to five value driver posts for every one promotional post. Don't look too 'selly' or it will turn off your audience.

When you don't know what to say but want to still post on Instagram.

79. Filed under: [activity, thing] to try ✨ (Display a great photo of an offbeat activity or act of self-expression.)

80. Another day, another [photo e.g. coffee] - can't get enough!

81. Use three emojis to describe [how you feel about this picture/your Friday/this week] We'll go first. [Emoji].

82. Post your 3 last most used emojis. Here's ours.

83. Happy hump day people! Here's a little something to get you through your Wednesday. [Post this on Wednesday]

84. Check out this incredible photo by [@person who posted photo] - Talk about inspiring.

85. Some serious [insert item] Inspo right here!

86. Brand crush alert: [Brand]. From their [something you love about them/what they are doing] to [another thing you love about them], we are totally digging what [name] and his/her team are doing. (This is a great shoutout for other brands that compliment your brand to notice you. Down the road you could maybe set up a cross-post promotion between both of your brands.)

87. Show us a more iconic [product, dynamic duo, person]. We'll wait. (Get creative and absurd with the imagery here)

88. So is it [something] or [something] (Two things that could get misconstrued). Asking for a friend.

89. The perfect [product, thing etc…] doesn't exi…… (Pair with a killer photo related to the caption)

90. Now this is a [holiday, season, day, style, house...] MOOD.

91. We believe in telling it like it is: No filters, no artificial anything. Just authentic [product offering]. [Post a unretouched BTS photo]

92. We're slaying the Monday blues by [how you're kicking ass on a Monday] - Your turn. Tell us how you are crushing your Monday!

93. An oldie but goodie. [Show an image of a past project for or from a client]

94. We went to this [event/networking/conference] during the [weekend/during] the week and it was super inspiring! Our biggest takeaways? [Highlight at least 3 learnings that you personally got from the event].

95. It's the simple things in life: [List some mundane things that bring a smile to your face? e.g. Old people holding hands].

96. One of the mantras we live by at [company/brand] is "[your favourite quote]". Why? Because [personal

reasons here].What's yours? Share some words of wisdom that inspire you.

.

97. Stay tuned, we are dropping something AMAZING on the blog in the next hour! You do not want to miss this!

98. 😭🙌 We're not worthy! (Post a screenshot of a five-star customer review of your product and show humble appreciation.)

99. Required inspiration: (Post an inspiring artwork image near the office) [Name of work] by [artist name]. [Description e.g. A 22 inch deep layer of dirt spread across a 3,600 sq ft gallery space in the middle of Soho, just a few doors down from our pop-up/office on Wooster St.]

100. THANK YOU! Here we are at the end of our first month. Thanks to everyone who's liked a gram, told a friend, or brought a [product] home.

💡 TIP

I never believed there is a formula for Instagram feeds and bios. But, I do think people make judgements about your brand within a split-second. So consider this: what do you want people notice about your page when they look at your overall feed? Is it clean and minimal? Bright and random? Or not thought out? In the bio, at the very least let people know who you are, what you do, and "why you?". Oh, and put your URL in there

The Importance of writing good copy.

So that's it!

It's worth to note that your competition is probably already posting content similar to yours. By using quality well-written captions, not only will you separate yourself/brand from the crowd, you will receive priceless brand loyalty from your customers.

The next time you find yourself at a loss for words, approach your copywriting from the angle of Instagram as a platform. It's used for building connection rather than just a sales pitch. Lastly, the visual factor of your posts is, of course, super important. It's what draws attention. In that respect, proper image and video curation are key.

Overall, posting without purpose serves as nothing more than an attention grab. Tell a story, write personal insights about you or your brand. Be as honest as possible and make the reader feel a part of that story. Maybe you're sharing a tip about running a marathon, a behind the scenes visit, or launching your first product. What experience have you personally had that inspired you to share this advice? Be genuine.

Without great copy to compliment your post you're losing out an opportunity to make more of an impact. That said, every once in a while it's ok to break the rule and post for post's sake but not recommended as a consistent strategy.

You will always get far more traction with a clear message. Thank you for supporting this book!

Good luck!

www.ingramcontent.com/pod-product-compliance
Lightning Source LLC
Chambersburg PA
CBHW030557220526
45463CB00007B/3102